This is a book that every Martial Arts school owner must read!

Hello, this is Jim Butin.
After 47 years running a highly
successful Martial Arts school,
I developed many proven concepts on
how to maximize the profit margins
of my school.

If you currently own a school, or are
considering opening one and want to
maximixe the profit potential...

this is the book for you.

Black Belt Karate Association, Inc.
was purchased by Jim Butin in October
of 1974 and renamed and incorporated
in 1988 to National Karate, Inc.and
re-incorporated as National Karate and
Tae Kwon Do, Inc. in 2013.

For the 47 year history of my school the
slogan that I used to state the purpose
of the business was:

"We specialize in classes for the beginner
and children."

Grand Master 10th Degree Black Belt

Jim Butin

beyondthefighting.com

JIM BUTIN
BEYOND THE FIGHTING

A guide to Business Strategy & Marketing Ideas for Martial Arts Schools

Five Reasons Why You Should NOT Allow Billing Companies to run Your EFT's (Electronic Fund Transfers)

Jim Butin owns and operates National Karate Inc. in Oklahoma City, Oklahoma and has maintained an in house EFT program since 1988

When a karate business uses agreements for payment, collection of the payments become a critical part of the success system.

#1 - Keep your Money!

The most obvious reason is that your profit will increase!

The argument for letting the billing company do it, is so that you can use your energy for more important projects.

What is more important than keeping as much of your money as possible in a down economy or a great economy?

If you have so many accounts and so many members that you can't keep track of them, then I might suggest that you develop or purchase a system to service these account better!

If you have 500 accounts, bringing in $100. per month per account, which seems to be a low dollar number by most industry standards, then you are paying somebody 3 to 5% (maybe more!) to collect your $50,000 monthly. That equates to $1,500 to $2,500 monthly or up to $30,000 per year to do something that you or a trusted employee can be trained to collect on the computer.

If you are a typical martial arts school owner, then you may only be servicing 50 to 150 members. These numbers allow you to have a hands on approach for controlling your own member electronic fund transfer debit's once or twice per month with a low amount of time needed to process the ACH's.

#2 - It's Too Complicated, you can't Figure it Out!

If you can turn on a computer, you can run your own accounts!

Look around, have you noticed how many banks are going away? The ones that are left must be more competitive to stay afloat in these harder financial times.

If your bank does not offer an ACH program for EFT's which include software and a FREE training program on how to implement and support for problems that you encounter, then you should call around to other financial institutions and move your accounts.

The cost of soft ware programs will vary, but FREE is the starting number. The average time to transact a 50 account ACH is approximately 30 minutes. Keep a file by your computer to file notes on cancellations that you want to enact, new accounts that you need to add, moving to inactive or back to active and upgrades to increase rates on existing accounts.

#3 - Change Your Rates or Payment Terms at any time!

You Operate a Service Business, Don't You?

What about offering your members an INACTIVE option on your membership payments if they encounter a family problem? Don't advertise it, but offer it if a problem arises. Maybe a family member has fallen ill or has an injury that will not allow participation in your classes.

Some owners may allow for early membership termination, and that sounds like you care for the member's problem, but it also is a loss of income. Why not offer a reduction in the membership to $9.99, or more, for up to three months, and a return to the regular rate at the end of that period, or sooner, if they can return for classes. This could apply to baseball season, summer vacation, trips away, or any other issue that might arise.

Of course you would like for them to come in at least once a week if possible, and you may reduce your program for that option as a temporary solution.

The longer that they are away, the less likely they are to return to your classes, EVER! At NKI we offer an open ended program with all of our memberships, yes, we have a cash price for a 12 or 36 month program, but we do not require re-enrollment to a higher membership at the expiration of the AGREEMENT. We are always working to upgrade memberships to Black Belt or Masters Programs, but if the upgrade does not happen, their membership rolls to month to month at the expiration of the term. Consequently, we have members that enrolled in 1988 that are still paying dues on their program. I have not heard of anyone, outside of our program, who effectively monitor or even offer this Inactive service to their members. Since you control the EFT, you can reduce or increase the amounts debited at any time. You don't have to spend time on the phone, on terminal hold, trying to talk to a real person about making a change or changes to your accounts.

#4 - You Keep Control of your Money!

You won't have to wait for a middle man to send your money to you!

With electronic banking, you don't have to wait for a check in the mail, your money is in the account the next day! Most billing companies wire directly to your account, but if you are still taking payments over the counter from your members, you are spending too much time on collection and not enough time on your other programs.

Don't be soft on requiring 100% participation on automatic withdraw. In fact you can offer a discount for using it, $129.00 per month by EFT or $149.00 over the counter. At NKI we explain that the only way we can process a monthly payment is by EFT or by credit card with numbers kept on file and processed monthly, if you choose not to pay in full. We are kick and punch guys, not accountants, to provide an effective service for our clients we must collect by these methods!

#5 - You Will Not Be Locked Into a Term of Participation!

You Can Experiment with $ Amounts, Number of Monthly Payouts, Open Ended Agreements!

Have you ever wondered whether a special 9 month membership or a Monthly Private Lesson Agreement might help you be more successful?

Most Billing companies prefer standard terms of collection and may charge extra fees for changes to your billings and or cycles. A Billing Company may even require an agreement for a specific amount of time that you must use their services, or monthly payment minimums to maintain.

When you call the shots, no one has to be notified and there are no penalties.

The Big Three Revenue Streams that Martial Arts Schools Never Use!

UNUSED Revenue Stream #1 – Karate Candy Fundraiser

Parents often ask "How can I afford tuition, belt exam fees, seminars, equipment and supply costs, and tournament events that the school is hosting?"

A simple solution exists to this commonly asked question in every karate school in the nation. Develop a fundraiser that benefits your students directly! Most fundraisers have kids selling items from which the money goes into a pool to purchase the item for the school that would benefit everyone. A great concept, but most kids and parents won't support such a broad and open based scenario of benefit year after year in the martial arts business!

Solution, develop a fundraiser that benefits each student directly! Why not have boxes of candy that can be checked out by a parent for a child to sell? The 30 bar box of candy can be purchased from Sam's Club for around $12.00 a box. The child then sells the candy at $1.00 or more per bar, he then turns in the $30.00 to you. You credit the child, or parent, with the $18.00 profit that may be used for belt exams, special events, team uniforms, or any of the extra revenue streams that your school is involved with. The owner wins big time because the money is being spent in the karate school and you are out nothing because the candy money cost is taken out off the top. The owner is in possession of the money before it has been spent, insuring that it won't be spent somewhere else. The student wins because, who is not strapped for cash with all of the rising costs that we are experiencing? Now the student will be able to participate in events or make purchases that increase the profitability of the karate school.

If you don't want to sell candy, how about candles, or pizza?

Choose other items that may be purchased wholesale and retailed at a profitable rate. It's a win-win deal for both the student and the karate school owner. Another huge benefit! Who is holding the money if a student should drop out or just does not use his "credit"?

Don't Give Cash, Give "Karate Bucks"!

Another rarely used concept that will be extremely beneficial to retaining profit and increasing sales in a martial arts school is the use of "Karate Bucks".

These Prizes are printed in different denominations. Give "Karate Bucks" for a referral, a friend brought in for Buddy Day, to participants of your next birthday party, as an additional prize in your next in-school tournament or event, etc.

QUESTION: How Do I get my Students to spend their money in my Pro-Shop instead of getting their Equipment On-Line?

Where are they going to spend these "Karate Bucks"? Most places don't honor them, but your place does! Accept them for all monthly events that you host, belt exams, equipment purchases, etc. That means more retail sales and profit for the Karate school. Require that the denomination of the Karate Bucks be used on items totaling twice the value and the worst you can do is break even if you charge twice the cost on all of your retail!

UNUSED Revenue Stream #2
Belt Advancement Packages

Even if you choose "Not " to charge for belt exams, you have to look at this opportunity to increase your retail sales. Would you prefer that your students buy one t-shirt or ten?

Do you have foam hand targets, kicking paddles and jump ropes available for students to use hanging on the wall? Or would you like to sell one to every member testing to your 1st colored belt and know that they are happy to have it?

In 2005 I implemented a structure for Belt Advancement Packages to increase my retail sales profits and cut out the opportunity for my students to spend their money for items, that I supply for sale, over the internet or in area athletic department stores. I took several steps to establish a logical transition into this plan.

First I sent a letter to my membership giving them the good news.

"Your tuition rates are not going to be raised! However, with increased business costs, escalating rent and fuel costs, National Karate Inc. is implementing a new Belt Advancement Package program to off set cost increases. You or your child will be given the items he will need in the next level of instruction on his next belt exam and your test fees will reflect these retail items."

Next I determined what items that I would include on each belt exam.

Gold Belt – NKI t-shirt (I now have a different colored shirt and logo for every belt level. Each of my students will own at least 10 NKI t-shirts by advancement to Black Belt), Hand held target, belt, diploma. $95.00 ($50. exam fee, $45.00 equipment + sales tax)

Orange Belt – NKI t-shirt, sparring gear, belt, diploma $249.00

Green Belt – NKI t-shirt, jump rope, kicking paddle, body protector, belt, diploma $150.00 and so on, you get the idea!

By the time a member takes the Black Belt exam he owns a wave master, kicking shield, re-breakable boards, NKI team uniforms, Instructor uniforms, and any other retail item that we may wish to include as required equipment.

Next I developed an info sheet, given at enrollment and made available before each belt exam, with a detail of the items included in the exam and the cost for the items. I include discounts for members on Black Belt Club programs, which helps in the up sell to that program also.

The bottom line:

- In 2004 I generated $9,000. (average of $45.00 per test) in income from belt tests without the Belt Advancement Packages.
- In 2005 I generated $20,300. (average of $105.00 per test) income from this system. In 2004 I sold 0 Century hand held targets,
- In 2005 I sold 65 because they were included in the testing equipment, do the math. Belt Advancement Packages are another revenue stream that most instructors are not using.

There is always room for adjustment, if a member tells me that he already has a Wave Master striking target, I inform him that I will reduce the cost of the target from his Purple Belt Advancement package. The good news is retail sales are up!

UNUSED Revenue Stream #3
Different In House Competitions for increased retention and profits!

QUESTION: When was the last time that your students **THANKED YOU** for encouraging them to attend large competitive events where they find that the face contact rules don't apply to them when they are hit, events where they have the opportunity to be cheated by bad officiating, be forced to sit on uncomfortable bleachers and waste their week-end with long waits due to inefficient tournament organization and spend a lot of money with rising gas costs and other associated expenses?

ANSWER: Never! And there go Your Retention Statistics, When your students QUIT because of Bad Experiences!

In 1993, I started the *"Kamikaze Karate Championships"* at National Karate as an in house event and catered the competition toward the most populated area of the school and the most profitable because of heightened excitement about the Martial Arts, the BEGINNER! Not only beginning kids 6 to 12, but towards the area that no other Karate events try to include, ages 3 to 5! I still offer these events every three months!

Think Out of the Box!

Observe your kids before or after class, do they ever pick up targets and try to slam each other? It must be fun if they are doing it, because the main objective for all kids is *"To Have Fun"! I turned this observation into "Sumo Battle"*.

Jim Butin's Sumo "Battle Basic" Rules

In the sparring ring, start from the go lines 6 feet apart, wear a head gear for safety (use different colors for winner identification), put a cargo strap around the kids and strap them to a Century Blast Master (so they will not use their arms to accelerate the impact of the push to increase safety) No time limit, start the match and let them push each other until: a) One goes out of bounds   b) One falls or touches his pad to the floor   c) Two wins are required to progress to the next round! Designed for beginners not ready for sparring ages 3 to 12 – Many of those who do spar will want to join in this fun event!

Jim Butin's One Legged Hop Fighting!

What else might be fun to a kid? How about "One Legged Hop Fighting"? No kicking or punching is allowed! In the sparring ring, start from the go lines, wear a head gear for safety, grab a rubber ring (we use the Century black stretch ring popular in Aerobic Kickboxing resistance classes), grab your own ankle, wear knee pads if you don't have a padded surface, falling on your knee on a concrete floor could result in injury and we don't need that, start the match! No time limit, shake and pull and hop until your opponent: a) Hops out of bounds b) Lets go of the ring, the one still holding the ring, wins. c) Falls or puts his foot down. d) Two wins are required to progress to the next round! Designed for beginners not ready for sparring ages 3 to 12 – Many of those who do spar also will want to join in this fun event!

Throwing Star and Blowgun Competition!

Have you ever been to a State Fair? What else might be fun to a kid? Is there a single 8 year old kid on the planet who would not like to have an opportunity to throw a "Star" or use a Blowgun? Even three year olds can throw a star or blow on the blowgun and fire a dart into an 8' styro-foam board with numbers placed on it for points scored, or pictures of black belts who have fallen from grace in your studio, for point value to win the awards you give!

At National Karate we alternate between these two divisions for every tournament. No time limit, shoot or throw five darts or stars at the target, move the starting line closer or farther away from the target as the age of the children require. Winners advance to the next round! Designed for everyone! All kids and many adults will want to join in this fun event!

Oh Yeah! Don't forget those other events: Sparring and Forms!

You know what to do here, so just do it! A suggestion for happier competitors, require pre-registration it makes your event more efficient and organized because you can chart the divisions in advance of the event, give each competitor an award for 1st, 2nd or 3rd based on their individual performance – 1st = Excellent, 2nd = Average 3rd = Weak (you will be amazed at how much faster your event will run!) Use this plan for all form divisions, breaking and self defense divisions. Pre-registration also allows you to pin point exactly how many awards that you will need for the event, therefore eliminating excess dollars spent on too many awards.

In 40 Years of Competing, Teaching and Hosting Events!

I have NEVER had a parent stop me after "The Old School Way" of hosting Karate Tournaments and say "Thank you, for this event, my child has benefited so greatly from today's competition! Bless you for your efforts!" NOW, I DO get this response almost every time we have an event! The Old School Way usually resulted in profanity, threats and lost students with bad experiences. We still offer the traditional Forms, Weapons and Sparring. But the "New Competition Events" represent a new direction in a new century that help retention and increase revenues!

Section 3
10 Reasons Why the Pay Per Class Program Is Superior!

Bill Clark, one of the most noted giants in the martial arts industry said "Maybe you are not doing it right!" in reference to the standard 12 month membership sales platforms that most studios use. One of his recent seminars conducted at the MAIA Super Show in Las Vegas examined the alternate choice of a per class membership. This article is based on this concept as developed by Jim Butin in Oklahoma City for National Karate & Tae Kwon Do, Inc.

1) The Sell is easy when you compare monthly with class hours sale!

When a potential new member contacts you to join he will ask, *"How much is it monthly?"* To which I will respond that *"You are not paying a monthly fee for classes, instead you are purchasing a number of classes for you or your child to participate in to develop martial arts skills. The more classes that you purchase will give you higher skills and you can always add on additional classes to your membership. You may pay for the program in full or pay in monthly installments with no interest or finance charges."*

2) Advantages for the Buyer. If you close for holidays or inclement weather no one loses!

We are a service business, so show the buyer his advantage already built in to your program to aid the customer. *"We will create an attendance card for each member that will be date stamped each time that he attends a class."* If the student was not here for the whole month of January, because of bad weather, school projects, sickness, or other problems, then he did not lose anything because we did not stamp his attendance card, because no classes were used. That makes it better than a monthly fee program. *"If you were on a monthly program and you did not attend, you will feel like you wasted your money because you did not attend!"*

3) Offer 2 or more options to pay off program monthly!

"How am I charged for the classes?" Our "Top" membership is the 300 hour Black Belt program, with ten belt levels and 30 classes between each of the belt levels. That program is $15.00 per class and you may set up a monthly payment schedule with no interest or finance charges on a bank EFT or credit card debit monthly until it is paid off. Then you will attend and use the 300 classes until they are used up! The suggested monthly payment is 30 payments of $150.00 per month, but you may choose a shorter term on payments or pay it off in one amount by credit card and pay the credit card company back at any monthly amount that you choose!

A customer might respond with, *"That may be too long a program for my child!"* Then you may choose our 90 hour Basic membership at $20.00 per class, which includes three levels of advancement to an intermediate level of skill in approximately 12 months to accomplish. You may attend up to three times per week, but at twice a week, which is the average, we would estimate that your membership will conclude in approximately that period of time, factoring in bad weather, vacations, baseball season, etc.

4) You have the power and flexibility to create variable hour membership offers!

Do you want to offer a sale or a special to your existing members when your statistics show you that a weak month is coming? Why not offer a 30 class option for $30.00 a session or a 60 class option at $25.00 a session. You could go the other way and charge $15 for the 30 class program and $10. For the 60 class extension, it is totally up to you. I tell people that I graduated from MSU, (Make Stuff Up!) so I know that you too can alter these options to fit your membership.

5) You can offer sales for upgrades anytime!

What is wrong with a "Black Friday" 50% off sale? National Karate did $24,500. In additional upgrades for the month of November 2014 with this sale. We did not make it a one day sale, which you could do, but instead we offered it for the whole month of November! Make the special drop from $15. To $10. Or $25 to $15. or whatever you feel is right for summer specials, Christmas specials, back to school specials, Easter, Labor Day specials, you choose the dates and the deals. It is always good to set your membership price high and then offer sales as "Specials" to encourage those upgrades or new sales to get the deal! We knew, at National Karate, that April and May are not particularly our strongest months of the year. So we established a "1,000 Class hour Sale". We advertised internally and on our website at nationalkarateinc.com. The rules were simple, purchase at least 20 classes or more at $10.00 per session until all of the 1,000 classes were gone. In six weeks we added $10,000 to our gross from existing members who wanted the reduced rate from $20.00 that they were paying per class on their existing membership. Purchases of 40, 50, 80 classes were common.

6) Your Students don't lose hours for time outs for other sports, or life!

We are a service business and with this plan you will be offering a huge advantage for the member. One point, that will help you to complete the sale when an objection rises from the customer, is to explain that we know that Joey will be in soccer, or football, or baseball, or is going on vacation, or will spend the summer with Grandpa and will not be around during certain times. As an owner, you will never have to add additional time to your members program. If he was not in class, you did not stamp his card, so the customer will not lose any of the hours on his program.

7) You can transfer class hours or share with family members easily!

If another family member would like to participate in classes, short term or longer, the hours can be shared. You will not have to write up a new agreement. The 300 hour program can be divided into 100 classes for three persons or 150 each for two persons. This accelerates the time in which the classes will be used up which promotes the need for more frequent upgrades, or reasons to upgrade when you offer a special sale on class hours.

You will not have to give discounts for additional family members at enrollment, and if you are charging $20. per class you are getting twice as much, or more, from participating family members. They will use up their classes sooner, which allows you to upgrade their membership as well.

If the member decides that he wants to quit and reasons that his child does not want to participate anymore, therefore he does not want to continue paying. Remind him that he owns a number of classes that can be sold or given to a neighbor, friend, or co-worker. It's like a car, it has value. Conclude your payment schedule and then if your child or another family member wants to come back in six months from now or longer, you can still use the classes purchased.

If you would prefer to sell your classes once they are paid off, we will accept a transfer and allow the new person to use the hours until concluded. After all as a school owner, don't you make money on belt exams, Mothers nights out, summer camps, in-house tournaments, equipment and gi sales and other activities that will gather more revenue from the new parties and don't they have new contacts that you may be able to get referrals from, and the opportunity to upgrade and add classes to their newly acquired program?

8) Increase your profit with additional clauses in your agreement!

If you are concerned that when a member discontinues his attendance that you have to maintain a record of the remaining hours on his membership forever? Then write in a maintenance agreement clause to your contract which will require a $10.00 monthly maintenance fee to go into effect after the standard expected time of 12 months or 36 months has ended. At enrollment we explain that this fee is optional, if the customer decides that he is not going to continue then he will lose the classes he has left, or he can pay the nominal fee monthly and use the classes in the future or sell, or give the classes to another and they can pay the fee.

At National Karate & Tae Kwon Do, Inc. I have three such clauses. One for the maintenance fee, one for mandatory participation in our four in house "Kamikaze" tournaments which we host each quarter. If you have not pre-registered for the event we will charge your account for the $40.00 entry fee, unless you have informed us that you have another commitment or are going to be out of the area at the time of the event. The benefit for the student is part of what our training is all about. Goal setting, sportsmanship, tenacity, responsibility and accomplishment are things that we include as reasons for participation in our events. If your member is one that you consider inactive and you do not want to charge them on their EFT or credit card, you could deduct 2 $20 classes from their class total to offset the charge.

The third clause pertains to the testing fees, which include equipment and supplies that you or your child is going to need in the next level of classes. Our test for Gold Belt includes a patch for your uniform, T-Shirt which may be worn instead of the gi top, belt and diploma, plus a hand held target for home use for $110.69 tax included. For Orange Belt the sparring gear is included in the testing for $262.00, etc. Since these items are covered at enrollment, parents seldom complain about the costs or requirements. If they have purchased items somewhere else or had the items given to them, we will not require that the purchase more, we just deduct those items from our testing charges.

9) Contests for additional Hours!

As an incentive for current members, create an opportunity to win additional hours to be added to your class times through referral contests, or perfect and constant attendance during the summer when a lot of students are lost. With good statistics, you know which month was the worst for last year. Our referral contest in June will award 5 class hours ($100.00) to each member who brings in a new person to join! Want more class hours? Bring more friends to join! Sounds like a great way to increase your revenue and enrollments for the summertime.

Very few schools have participated in this idea and they will not benefit as you will be able to do! Each November right after "Black Friday" has subsided, National Karate gives every member attending classes, beginner through advanced, a packet of five "Karate for Christmas" gift certificates. We typically give out 5 certificates to each member along with a cover letter explaining that National Karate wants to give every member $100. For Christmas.

To get your $100. You must give out all five certificates to friends, co-workers, neighbors, or other persons wanting to receive a ***FREE Karate For Christmas membership.**" When the person arrives at our studio to redeem his certificate the students name that is on the certificate gets credit for the new member. The value of each certificate is "$20 Karate Bucks", not cash, which may be applied to a belt exam, a monthly $30. "Ninja Night", our famous "Kamikaze Karate Championships" held three times per year, purchases of equipment totaling $40. or more, or in additional class hours that you can add to the members program.

10) Track the members hours used with an attendance card system!

Tracking is an issue! When each student lines up to start his class, each will have an attendance card that he has retrieved from our card file box. Everyone likes to feel that he is valuable and that others know him, use their name a lot, which is easy because of the card system. The card is collected as the class starts and helps our instructors learn the names of each of the kids or adults in class, and to know when they are to receive a stripe toward advancement. When the card has been date stamped, we know the date when he was in class last, how many classes he has left on his program, when to upgrade him to purchase more hours, and when he is eligible for his next belt exam. Use a software system to track attendance on your computer if you like, with a flag to notify you when there are 5 or 10 classes left on the memberships so that you can create a conference to add sessions to the membership .

We are constantly tweaking this concept and adding changes to our programs and selling of memberships. These points should start your thinking towards a different way to do things. Like Bill Clark said,
"Maybe you are not doing it right!"

Section 4

Five Superior Martial Art Marketing Ideas That Could Be the "Magic Bullet" For You

#1 Valentine Day Cards

You can't lose on this promotion, every kid must participate!

In all elementary schools Valentine's Day is a big deal! Many printing companies produce martial arts related valentine cards that you can modify to advertise your location and offer a FREE month (or shorter term) of martial arts classes to any child that participates.

All kids must bring valentine cards to every child in their class, so that we do not hurt any ones feelings!

This promotion means that you will have contact with every child that your existing student has in his homeroom. All that is necessary is that you produce the valentines in advance, probably in January, so that your students Moms don't go out to purchase valentine cards from another source. Advertise to your members that if they need additional cards, you have them available.

#2 Super Kids Day

This may be the best marketing tool of all time!

Do you want to have a relationship with elementary schools in your area?

Use this idea to get your foot in the door and get your schools to contact you for other activities.

In Oklahoma City, the Putnam City School district has a **"Super Kids Day"** usually scheduled for a Friday in May. This celebration is for all kids of the school and celebrates the end of the school year. Parent volunteers help with the day activities that are usually coordinated by the PE teacher.

The kids participate in face painting, bean bag toss and games all day. National Karate has participated in these events at several elementary schools and we are so appreciated that all of the schools call us to see if they can get on our schedule to participate. We bring out our "Ninja Zone" bounce house and supply head gear for safety so that the kids don't bang heads together and need medical attention or stitches. We also bring out our wooden breaking stand that we constructed, which will support re-breakable boards. We bring a set of sparring hand gear to help the little guys break the boards with no pain.

HOW DO WE BENFIT?

Each child that breaks a board (everyone) gets a certificate from our studio for a FREE month (or shorter term) of classes to be used during the summer. Place an expiration date, if you like, to create urgency and get a fast response, or simply allow the use of the certificate at any time of the year. We give 500 certificates to each school in bundles of 25. These certificates are given by each homeroom teacher to the kids at the end of the day. Figure it out, 6 elementary schools, with 500 kids per school, are currently on our participation list, that's 3,000 kids that we will be able to touch directly with our free marketing offer in our direct area within five miles of our location.

The cost?

Some printing, some rubber bands, and 6 days that we must attend the event from 9 am to 3 pm and conduct the board breaking and bounce house operation. The Putnam City School district requires that we place a printed disclaimer on each certificate to show non-recommendation of our business to the public. How else can you participate in a one day event and have direct contact with every child in your community. With this one idea, direct mail marketing is no longer important when you want to reach children 6 to 12. As a result of this idea, several PE teachers have contacted National Karate to ask for participation in other events! It's a win win.

#3 Karate for Christmas

December is typically one of the worst months of the year! *Unless you are prepared!* One of the ways to bring in a good amount of income is through a

"Karate Shopping Day". Most schools have learned to advertise this day well in advance and offer great values to help move out old inventory. Many expand the sale to be a week long or even for the whole month.

Experimentation will prove out which method is best for you!

Very few schools have participated in this idea and they will not benefit as you will be able to do! Each November right after "Black Friday" has subsided, National Karate gives every member attending classes, beginner through advanced, a packet of five "Karate for Christmas" gift certificates. We typically give out 5 certificates to each member along with a cover letter explaining that...

National Karate wants to give every member $100 For Christmas.

To get your $100. You must give out all five certificates to friends, co-workers, neighbors, or other persons wanting to receive a *"FREE Karate For Christmas membership."* When the person arrives at our studio to redeem his certificate the students name that is on the certificate gets credit for the new member.

The value of each certificate is **"$20 Karate Bucks"**, not cash, which may be applied to a belt exam, a monthly $30. **"Ninja Night",** our famous **"Kamikaze Karate Championships"** held three times per year, or purchases of equipment totaling $40. or more.

#4 Kinder Karate for ages 3 to 5

Have you ever had parents call you for their child at 4 years old to start training in karate. Only to answer with, *" I am so sorry, but we don't start kids in karate before the age of 6!"* I did, and after answering in such a fashion for about 100 times, it finally dawned on me that I was losing revenue by not having a program that would cater to this younger group and the demand that was obviously there.

I was not sure that I had the patience to deal with this younger faction, but decided to give it a try. After all, if I could not make the program work or lost too many brain cells, I could always discontinue the program. I decided to limit the class size to 8 kids age 3 to5. I could see that a larger class would be like trying to herd chickens into a box.

I also realized that I needed to have much lower expectations on their developing skills.

The program revolved around a shorter class time at 30 minutes. I started the class with our **"Martial Arts Creed"** (page 33) and asked who knew one part of it. Sometimes one or two hands would rise and when they recited their part we went on to the next of the 3. Everything was **"Yes sir"** and **"No sir"** and the parents loved it. They needed to, they are the ones that pay for it. If you do not have parents seated at the class area you are missing out on the easiest form of sales.

When you ask each child *"What did you do this week to help around the house?"* or *"Get to bed on time and eat everything that your Mom puts on your plate!"* You will see the parents nodding in approval. Add plenty of games and fun activity in the class, and make sure you include the concept that *"You can't win a fight, so do not be in one!"* Hit targets and pads but not each other. If someone pushes you or calls you a name, just walk away. But if they grab you and try to hurt you, you must stop them because no one has the right to hurt or injure you. You can charge monthly on this program or in three month or six month increments as you choose. The fees can be in tune with your other programs or more. Think about it, you are offering something that parents can't get anywhere else and something that can mold their child in a positive way that will stay with them for the rest of their lives. Another lesson I learned from McDonalds and their happy meals, it's all about the toy! I bought items from the dollar store, such as little dinosaurs, army men, and other trinkets and gave one to every child at the end of every class as a reward for their participation. It might just keep them coming back!

#5 Aerobic Kickboxing

Before Billy Blanks became so huge with "Tae Bo" I had developed an Aerobic Kickboxing program as an exercise program for women and men that may not be interested in karate classes, but were looking for an opportunity to improve their cardio and have fun using a martial arts exercise theme.

I divided our video into two sections, one was a **"Technique Video"** which taught the proper way to use the strikes on targets without injury and get the most out of the workout. The Second was the workout itself which comprised the action into warm up activity for about a third of the class, using the premise of **"Shadow Boxing"** with striking combinations with punches, knees and kicking motions. Then moving on to bag striking, using those same combinations on stand up water filled bags for another third of the class. Then encouraging a warm down period using crunches, jump rope and stretching exercises.

When offering this class to the public you have several options. You or an instructor can learn the combo's and run the class similar to the video that is available to you. I would suggest you charge a nominal fee for the first class and provide boxing gloves and the striking bags for the users. Maybe $8 to $10. Then apply that amount as a credit to the membership if they actually join. Another option is to have the video running at specific times when other classes are not going on and let the video run the class for participation by your members. Still another plan is to make the video available for purchase for your members along with an equipment package of the jump rope, wrist wrap gloves, or boxing gloves and Powerline Wavemasters available from Century for in home use.

Whichever method you use, you will find a new revenue stream for your studio that will attract people that you did not already have. Those Mom and Dad's that are in your studio all the time, could be contributing in revenue and participation on a family scale that you did not enjoy before.

Visit: http://beyondthefighting.com
to order **Butin Karate Aerobics Kickboxing Video**

SECTION #5

Section 5
Instructor Organization for better Teaching and Retention!
Calendar Rotating Curriculum Guide

Have you ever had students who complained that they could never come to "Sparring class or Fight night" because of other commitments? How about those who can never come on "Forms night". Does that give them a reason to not progress and consequently drop out of your program?

Would it be great if your students who come to class on Monday and Wednesday would share the same curriculum with those attending on Tuesday and Thursday?

In 1975 I developed a Calendar curriculum to handle a structure of rotating curriculum necessary to organize and systemize the necessary material that every student would need for advancement to the next higher level. The reason for implementation was simple, most every instructor will teach the things that he is good at, or interested in, not particularly the material that each student needs, or should learn on a systematic basis.

This system allows me, as the owner and employer of several instructors, the security to know that the curriculum is being covered for every level of student in my membership.

The Calendar format is simple:

1. Develop a curriculum guide of five lesson plans for each level of instruction in your membership.

As an example, for white belts class 1 may be: Front choke defense, front punch and back punch, Forward stance. Class 2 may be: Punch defense, Front snap kick, Rising block. (Each curriculum developer can enter in his own structure for itemizing these plans. Develop plans for each level of instruction, Beginning, Intermediate, and Advanced, or a set of lesson plans for every belt level in your program divided into 5 groups.)

2. Obtain a desk calendar with large squares for marking

3. Mark each square, Monday through Saturday, with a number in order 1 through 5, then repeat the process. (I exclude Sunday, most clubs are closed)

4. If properly marked, each day of the week will feature a different number 1 through 5 for the month listed. This equates to each lesson plan being covered for a specific day, such as Monday, for 5 straight Mondays. Each lesson plan will be covered for that day of the week and then the lesson plans will repeat.

5. Post the curriculum guide with the lesson plan curriculum on the wall next to the mounted desk calendar.

6. Now, each instructor can see which lesson plan is posted for that day and knows what material is to be covered. Each instructor may interject additional material if the base lesson plan is covered in less time than the class exists for, but this system insures that each student attending even just one consistent day a week (every Monday as an example) is sufficiently introduced to all of the material for his next belt advancement. For the student attending 2 or 3 times per week, he is getting the material more frequently.

As an owner, chief instructor, you now are able to relax your fears that some students may not be receiving all of the requirements that you want them to learn.

Section 6
External Marketing Ideas
Lessons to learn!

Have you ever experimented with television advertising? It is always an interesting topic, because our activity is so visual and most people have an image in their minds the instant that martial arts or "Karate" is mentioned.

One topic that you should always consider when you are constructing a video for the internet or television advertising is the concept of *"Black Belt Eyes!"*

The action or video that will fire you up and that you think will get everyone excited about your activity could backfire on you as it did to one of my special Black Belt friends in Wichita, Kansas. He made a 30 second commercial that showed his students throwing each other across the mat, kicking each other in the head, punching and getting punched, air getting knocked out of each other with kicks and punches to the body. Basically he showed all of the things that we know as instructors a person should be able to do to a bad guy! The things that he showed were things that we appreciate through "Black Belt Eyes" and that we hope all of our students develop the skills to do to another human being who may want to hurt you. The problem is that when Mom sees the ad, she thinks "There is no way I am going to let my child go in there and get hit like that!" Dad thinks, "Wow, if I go down there they are going to beat the crap out of me every day!"

People watching the video see themselves as being hit, not doing the hitting, so the violent video had the opposite effect than what the Karate school owner intended. He also added to the negative side of the display by adding, "You think Karate is tough, you don't know how tough it really is!" Not surprising most of us, he did not receive one phone call for inquiries or to enroll after running that television commercial several times.

Your ads should show people having fun and smiling, action against each other should show skills, but no damage, no crying, no blood, or injury. Instructors shaking hands and patting people on the back, a friendly environment where everyone is proficient, confident, respectful, and skilled. A place where you feel safe to walk in to.

Once you have developed the video to your satisfaction, you can include it on your website, purchase air time on cable networks or on television shows that have the audiences that you are seeking.

Another concept is through direct mail. You can create a special offer with your video that can be placed on a CD rom business card that can be sent to homes in your area using the demographics that are pertinent to your marketing plans to reach children or specific income parameters and zip codes close to you. There are companies through which you can purchase mailing lists to direct your marketing to make it the most profitable.

Section 7
Staff Motivation
A "Modified" Bible Parable for Karate School Owners

One recent evening, when I woke up with a splitting headache, either from the stress of running my karate business in Oklahoma City and the apparent failure to motivate my staff properly, or was it the onion rings and fried clams I cooked for dinner, it was probably the rings! I slid into my bathtub for a hot bubble bath, to relieve my headache along with some Excedrin at 5:00 am. While relaxing in the tub and thinking about my staff and the projects I had given them to work on since the last meeting, I deduced that they probably had not given the last meeting much thought, much less had attended to the projects.

Then I started to thank the Lord for all that I have and have accomplished in the martial arts and my life. I was then reminded of a story in the Bible that has given me a new tool to reach and motivate my staff. I will be using this parable, modified of course, in the next meeting that we have, and maybe you will too!

It will go something like this, Once there was a Karate instructor who had to go away for an extended period of time. He gathered his three staff members and informed them of his departure and told them of an opportunity that he was giving them. Each staff member would receive $1,000 each to use to increase the profitability of the Karate school while he was gone. He was away for a time and when he returned he gathered his staff together to find out the results of their efforts.

25

The first staff member said, *"Wow! Are you going to be happy!* I took the $1,000 and bought karate uniforms and sparring gear and weapons from Century Martial Arts Supply at a huge discount sale that they were having. I started a weapons class and sold all of the weapons I bought, plus I increased our sales of equipment at belt exams by offering them "Belt advancement packages" when they take their test for the next belt and offered them equipment that they will need in the next level. I started a new beginners self-defense program at the local church and sold all of the uniforms, and 50% of the new students came here to our school and joined on Black Belt Programs. I even took the referral program to the next level and personally talked to every current member and got three new leads per person that I intend to invite to class for intro programs!"

The second staff member said, *"Well, my news is not as great!* I took the $1,000 and bought advertising on television, even though you have told us it was not effective with one location. I also bought print advertising in the newspaper and some local satellite papers with a new student special, even though the print was run only one time and may have gotten limited viewing exposure as you have said. I even ran some radio spots on two of the most popular, high demographic stations in our area, but after spending all of the money, I only recouped about ½ of the $1,000 with the new students that have joined that responded to the advertising."

The third staff member stepped up and retorted, *"Man, my news is better than that! I knew it was a bad economy so I did not buy any advertising, because I knew it was a waste! I had too many things going on in my life, so I did not get any referrals from our members or sign up anyone new, because I knew someone else would do it*! No way would I spend the money on new equipment, because everybody here has some! So I just held on to the cash to return to you in full!"

So which staff member reflects your crew?

I wish I had two or three #1's, Hey! I would settle for just ONE! Anyway, I will continue to train and try to motivate others to do what I do and will continue to examine the Bible for other stories that could be "tweaked" to help me in my efforts! *And so should you!*

Section 8
Jr. Black Belt Rank Advancement

So Many Questions:

Many Karate school owners wonder what to do with the problems concerning Junior Black Belt testing. Do you test them the same as adults over the age of 18? Do you make their tests easier? Should they have the same status as an adult black belt. Is it fair to expect their test to be as demanding as an adult who has reached full growth and has achieved full balance and coordination since their bodies are mature?

And what about the growth that the younger students will experience, will their skills continue to develop as they get older or will they lose some skills because of body changes as they mature?

What if they do not stay active in the martial arts and their skills have deteriorated with age, should they be required to re-test for their rank? Do you make the younger students wait until they are 18 or older to test for Black Belt? Is it fair to make the younger students wait so many years to test?

Will they lose interest with no opportunity to advance and drop out of your program because of it?

The requirements that you may use for Black Belt testing do not need to be altered, just use this format for generating a fairer and separate testing plan for your students ages 6 to 17. At National Karate the policy is to have three distinct age group levels and to make them visually distinctive from each other, but still carry the status of being at the top of their skill levels based on age.

In National Karate's belt rank system, we use 3 levels of adult Brown belt testing, 4th then 3rd then 2nd and test to 1st red belt. We then modify the junior testing to Black Belt White stripe instead of 3rd brown.

Martial arts suppliers have black belts available for purchase with a continuous white stripe, brown stripe or red stripe in the center of the belt to complete the designation of a junior level. The requirements that we use are equal to the requirements for an adult testing to the 3rd degree brown belt level.

Eligibility for Advanced Stripe Testing

Black w/White Stripe Instead of 3rd Brown . . . . .Ages 11 & under

Black w/Brown Stripe Instead of 2nd Brown . . . . Ages 12 to15

Black w/Red Stripe Instead of 1st Red . . . . Ages 15 to 17

Jr. Black Belt Rank Advancement

An Order for advancement to 2nd and 3rd Degree Black Belt for Juniors

Your form requirements will be different than those used at National Karate based on your style and structure. Feel free to make any adjustments to the items on our required list. These are only suggestions to help you create a positive structure for advancement.

JR. Black Belt White Stripe Instead of 3rd Brown

Age 11 and under
The requirements that you use for 3rd brown are the ones that we suggest for this test advancement!
We currently require these students to wait until they are 12 to test for their next Black Belt Level. Lack of reward will probably cause most students to lose interest and quit. We now will offer incentives to test for 2nd and 3rd degree Black Belt in these age groups.

2nd Degree – Test is available in 1/3 of the time of the candidates age in relation to Age 12 and Green Stripe testing when White stripe testing was completed. Plus these requirements:

Sparring Requirement – 4 matches

Breaking Requirement – Green re-breakable board by kick

Form Requirement – Tosan, Yul Gok

Knife Defense – Front Touch, Back Touch, Rear Throat

Self Defense - Front Choke, Collar Grab & Punch, Rear Choke

Tournament Participation - 4 required events

(Special Tournament Stripe placed on belt once earned)

28

3rd Degree – *Test is available in 2/3 of the time of the candidates age in relation to Age 12 and Green Stripe testing when White stripe testing was completed. Plus these requirements:*

Sparring Requirement – 5 matches

Breaking Requirement – Blue re-breakable board by kick

Form Requirement – Tan Gun, Tosan, Yul Gok

Knife Defense - Back Touch, Rear Throat, Overhead Stab

Self Defense - Rear Bear Hug Side Head Lock, Wrist Grab

Tournament Participation - 4 required events + One additional

JR. Black Belt Brown Stripe Instead of 2nd Brown

Age 12/13/14
The requirements that you use for 2nd brown are the ones that we suggest for this test advancement!

We currently require these students to wait until they are 15 to test for their next Black Belt Level. Lack of reward will probably cause most students to lose interest and quit. We now will offer incentives to test for 2nd and 3rd degree Black Belt in these age groups.

2nd Degree

Test is available at 13. Plus these requirements:

Sparring Requirement – 6 matches

Breaking Requirement – Blue re-breakable board by kick

Form Requirement – Yul Gok, Wha Rang

Knife Defense –   Back Touch, Rear Throat, Slash Attack

Self Defense - Front Choke, Collar Grab & Punch, Rear Choke

Tournament Participation - 4 required events

3rd Degree – Test is available at 14.
Plus these requirements:

Sparring Requirement – 7 matches

Breaking Requirement – Brown re-breakable board by kick

Form Requirement – Yul Gok, Wha Rang

Knife Defense – Back Touch, Rear Throat, Slash Attack

Self Defense - Front Choke, Collar Grab & Punch, Rear Choke

Tournament Participation - 4 required events + One additional

JR. Black Belt Red Stripe Instead of 1st Red
Age 15/16/17 -

The requirements that you use for 1st brown or red belt are the ones that we suggest for this test advancement!

We currently require these students to wait until they are 18 to test for their next Black Belt Level. Boredom and lack of reward will probably cause most students to lose interest and quit. We now will offer incentives to test for 2nd and 3rd degree Black Belt in these age groups.

2nd Degree – Test is available at age 16.
Plus these requirements:

Sparring Requirement – 8 matches

Breaking Requirement – Brown Re-breakable board plus one by kick

Form Requirement – Tosan, Yul Gok, Wha Rang

Knife Defense – Front Touch, Back Touch, Rear Throat

Self Defense - Front Choke, Collar Grab & Punch, Rear Choke

Tournament Participation - 4 required events + 2 Additional

3rd Degree – Test is available at age 17.
Plus these requirements:

Sparring Requirement – 9 matches

Breaking Requirement – Black re-breakable board plus one by kick

Form Requirement – Yul Gok, Wha Rang, Choong Mu

Knife Defense - Back Touch, Rear Throat, Overhead Stab

Self Defense - Rear Bear Hug Side Head Lock, Wrist Grab

Tournament Participation - 4 required events + 2 Additional

Adult Black Belt

Age 18 to 35

Test requirements for this level will be custom designed for the applicant

Senior Adult Black Belt

Age 35 & Up

Test requirements for this level will be custom designed for the applicant

Proposed Ranking Structure

Youth Age 11

White 10th, Gold 9th , Orange 8th – Beginner levels

Green 7th , Blue 6th , Purple 5th – Intermediate levels

Brown 4th - Black Belt White Stripe 1st, 2nd and 3rd - Advanced levels

These suggestions are designed to help with retention and continued involvement in your membership, feel free to alter or change the format, but the concept should improve your program.

Youth Ages 12 to 14

White 10th, Gold 9th , Orange 8th – Beginner levels

Green 7th , Blue 6th , Purple 5th – Intermediate levels

Brown 4th , 3rd - Black Belt Brown Stripe 1st, 2nd and 3rd - Advanced levels

Youth 15 to 17

White 10th, Gold 9th , Orange 8th – Beginner levels

Green 7th , Blue 6th , Purple 5th – Intermediate levels

Brown 4th , 3rd, 2nd - Black Belt Red Stripe 1st, 2nd and 3rd - Adv levels

Adults 18+

White 10th, Gold 9th, Orange 8th – Beginner levels

Green 7th, Blue 6th, Purple 5th – Intermediate levels

Brown 4th, 3rd, 2nd - Red 1st - 1st Black – Advanced levels

The Martial Arts Creed

By far the best student retention tool!

It is guaranteed that if a parent hears their child recite the Martial Art Creed in class, they will understand the importance of this training,

Many schools have gone away from using this important creed. Bring it back! It works!

In my studio, we took great pride in working on all kids to have a great attitude and develop responsibility, and respect for others. There are benefits to the martial arts training for everyone, even if they never use their martial art skills in a self- defense situation. We required our kids repeat our Martial Arts Creed every day in every class.

Honesty in the Heart, means don't lie, don't steal, don't cheat, do things to help your friends, neighbors, and family every day. We then would ask every child about what they did previously to help their family. If they did nothing to help, the instructor would then ask the class, *"What do you think this guy should do here right now, because he did nothing to help his family?"* I would then ask the class. *"Should we set his hair on fire?, Should we body slam him? Or should he do 10 push ups?"* The push up option was the obvious choice, but the possible punishment for doing nothing to help was a great deterrent to establish a reason to help around the house and create family participation. Many times parents would report to me that their child would come and ask them what they could do to help around the house. The parent would be excited that their child thought ahead to make sure they were not going to have to do extra sit ups or push ups when they came to class! The parent was doubly excited to realize that their child was now interested in helping around the house because of this requirement that National Karate had implemented.

Strength in the Body, means no drugs, no smoking, no alcohol, get to bed on time and eat everything your Mom puts on your plate! Many times I had heard a Mom tell me that because of our Creed, all she had to say was. *"I know someone at the karate studio who will want to hear that you did not*

33

eat your vegetables!" That was effective, and it sure does not hurt to have a discussion about drugs and alcohol to children by people other than parents or school officials. The importance of good role models in your child's life is immeasurable. Television constantly sends the wrong messages about how to deal with others, how to live your life, treat your family, or do what you want no matter what others may think!

Your child will respect the karate instructor because he should demand it!. Answering **"Yes sir" and "No sir"** is a great way to start. A good karate instructor will insist on this response.

This should be maintained in the home as well. You love your child, but he is not your buddy! He must do what you say to maintain discipline.

Knowledge in the Mind, means listen to your teacher, get your

homework done on time and make the best grades that your school gives out. I required that all of our kids brought in their report cards to show me. If their grades were above average they then would qualify to get a red stripe on their belt. If a child brought me two good report card reports in a row, the child would then earn an "Academic Achievement" patch for their uniform. Kids who saw these awards given out wanted them and would try harder in school so that they could earn one. It's a win-win deal! To help establish responsibility in every child, they must understand that it gets done because they do it. If they don't stand up to a bully, or take the trash out, or turn in their assignment, the end result is always accountable to them.

This martial arts creed will develop respect, responsibility and discipline when it is adhered to on a consistent basis.

It is widely known, but not very well advertised, that the martial arts as a physical activity for children is probably the top exercise program for developing the core values of self-worth in children and adults.

Character Development Through Martial Arts

Not only is emphasis placed on the Martial Arts Creed in our program at National Karate for our beginning kids, but we continue their education as they advance into the higher rank structure. The establishment of the 10 Martial Arts Codes of Conduct are designed to expand the requirements of all of our progressing students to be aware that their contribution to family and community extends past the basic Martial Arts Creed. The requirements for further belt advancement include knowing three of the "Codes of Conduct" to advance to Orange belt, five of the codes to progress to Blue belt and seven of the codes to make it to Purple belt and all 10 of the codes to examine to Brown belt and higher. These codes should be a part of every family's education for their children and they have been the basic foundation for our youth in America. For some unknown reason these values are not stressed or maintained in the school system anymore or in most American families.

The #1 Code is to address sir or ma'am to all elders. Respect should be given from every child to elders and if we do not require it, who will?

The #2 Code is to bow when entering and leaving the gym floor. Our respect extends outside of the adult appreciation arena into the areas that contribute to us in a special way! When we started our training we knew nothing, every time we leave the floor we have had an opportunity to learn more and progress in our skills. So every time we leave or advance into this area requires a certain understanding of respect for what is about to happen or for what just happened!

The #3 Code is to bow to your instructor at the 1st meeting of each day and before asking a question. This could be related to a respect for authority, but most certainly for the one who directs you and cares about the progress that you intend to make to improve yourself in the Martial Arts world.

The #4 Code is to practice 3 polite greetings to your parents each day. When you wake up, when you come home from school, and when you retire for the evening. Family should be the most important thing to you and showing appreciation and respect to your family is not only required by the Bible, but should be reinforced always!

The #5 Code is to accept corrections from parents and teachers cheerfully! If a parent or teacher did not care about you he would not say anything about an incorrect answer or response. Because he wants to see you be the best you can be, he or she will always seem to be trying to correct you, so do not take it as a negative thing. Just smile and say *"Yes ma'am, I will try harder!"*

The #6 Code is to obey your conscience, not your instinct! Your instinct is selfish and wants you to take something that is not yours or to the thing that you know is wrong. Your conscience knows what is right and will always direct you toward the proper decision.

The #7 Code it to be loyal to your friends. Sometimes in a peer group, there will be those who make fun of or talk badly about others. Stand up for your friends and don't allow negative talk to be used about them. Especially when they are not there to stand up for themselves.

The #8 Code is to honor your country. We live in the greatest country in the world and there are plenty of detractors out in our society who are slandering our way of life and our leaders. We are not in a perfect society, but we can't improve the way things are by doing things in a negative way, instead contribute to make things better.

The #9 Code is to always try your best at anything that you do in sports or academics. If it is worth doing, do it right. Train hard to be the best you can be in the Martial Arts and gain wisdom through studying hard and expanding your mental horizons.

The #10 Code is to find happiness through truthful living. Live your life in an honest and truthful way and strive to be happy. Our lives are short and to see each day as a blessing is a great way to affect the lives of others and to create a positive impact on others around you.

What parents have to say about the benefits of the training:

Many parents have contacted me long after their kids have finished in their pursuit of belt advancement and personal successes in the martial arts to inform me how valuable they believe the martial arts had been toward the maturation of their children.

Section 9
Get involved in the WMARA!

MEMBER

Many Karate school owners are affiliated with a ranking organization or have involvement with their instructor for certification of their students rank. Unfortunately, many instructors find themselves on an island when it comes to certification for their own rank if their instructor has quit the martial arts or he is disassociated for another reason. Or maybe an instructor would like to be a part of a larger organization that has increased credibility and that may encourage participation from others to join their membership!

The World Martial Arts Ranking Association was developed by pioneer and 1st National Black Belt Champion J Pat Burleson.

His vision.....

The new affiliate WMARA program will add revenue to your business, by offering a return of $5. from the initial $25. yearly membership fee and it will be returned to you for each of your students who join the organization.

Not only will your students enjoy the prestige of being a part of this great organization, but they also will receive, membership sticker and patch, as well as blogs and e-mails concerning upcoming events and testing of higher rank Black Belts.

Request an application for an affiliate membership for your martial arts studio to:

Jim Butin – WMARA Director at beyondthefighting@gmail.com

Visit: https://beyondthefighting.com/wmara

The endorsers of the WMARA program are indeed the most respected icons in the Martial Arts industry. Each one has given Master J. Pat Burleson permission to use their names and endorsement to the advancement of all Black Belt Ranks as if they personally attended each testing event. Several of these icons are deceased and it will be impossible for anyone to obtain the approval of them from any other organization.

Steve Armstrong – Steve was a practitioner of Okinawan Isshin Ryu was an author of Isshin ryu Kata books and established Martial Arts instruction in his 1st Northwest United States karate school in 1960.

J. Pat Burleson – The 1st National Black Belt champion acquired in 1964 in Washington DC – Pat is the founder of the WMARA and had the vision to establish an organization remembering the icons of the martial arts in America and combining that with the opportunity for others to be a part of the history and receive the greatest benefits that can be acquired by so many in our industry.

Dr. Maung Gyi – A practitioner of Bando and Burmese Martial Arts – Dr. Gyi formed the American Bando Association and was the chef instructor of the USKA, He was the chief referee of the PKA in 1976 and other distinguished organizations. For the US and Europe he was chairman of the rules and regulations committee for Black Belt magazine, he promoted Bando free fighting and kickboxing championships in the United States.

Jim Harrison – A practitioner of Karate, Judo, Aiki Jutsu, and Kickboxing. Jim had exceptional success in law enforcement and ran a successful Martial Arts school in Kansas City and moved to Missoula, Montana where he continued to train the public. Jim was highly sought after for seminars and as a Karate competitor was the man that no one wanted to fight. He won numerous National Black Belt Championships, fought in the earliest kickboxing shows and his warrior spirit was reflected in his Bushido-Kai Dojo daily.

Gene LeBell – Boxing, wrestling, Karate, and Judo – Gene has authored 12 books and worked in Hollywood as a stunt coordinator in numerous movies and worked with Bruce Lee, Chuck Norris and others, He is and ex-champion in wrestling and Judo and is highly respected by martial artists all over the world.

Joe Lewis – Okinawan Shorin Ryu Karate and 1st US Kickboxer – He formed the Joe Lewis American Karate System in 1967. He was the 1st PKA Heavyweight World champion in Kickboxing established in 1974. Joe was a devastating fighter and won most of the top karate tournaments of the day numerous times.

Chuck Norris – Tang Soo Do, Brazilian Jiu Jitsu, American Karate, and Judo – Chuck is an American Martial Artist, actor, film producer, and screen writer. He starred with Bruce Lee in "Return of the Dragon", and in numerous successful films, and starred in the "Walker, Texas Ranger" television series. Chuck is an author of several books and was an accomplished tournament competitor and has won numerous black belt championships. He is the founder of "Kickstart" a non profit organization designed to aid middle school children with the benefits of martial arts training.

Edmond Parker – Father of American Kenpo – Ed opened the 1st Kenpo dojo in 1956 in Pasadena, California and taught American Kenpo Karate which included influences from judo and several karate styles. An accomplished author, Ed hosted the 1st International Karate Championships in Long Beach, Ca. in 1964.

Jhoon Goo Rhee – Father of American Tae Kwon Do – He introduced TKD in 1956 in Texas. He was also an actor in several films and had an extensive presence in Washington, DC with several schools and a huge list of successful Black Belt competitors.

Allen Steen – American Karate – One of the top competing karate tournament pioneers of the "Blood and Guts" era of tournament karate, Mr. Steen established a karate business empire of schools in Dallas, Texas starting in 1962. Many of the elite martial arts competitors trace their origins to Allen Steen.

Robert Trias – Father of American Martial Arts and founder of the USKA – Master Trias was an author and wrote the 1st rules and ran the 1st karate tournament in the US in 1955. He established the United States Karate Association in 1948.

Bob Wall – Okinawan Martial Arts, Tang Soo Do Karate, Jiu Jitsu – Bob was an actor with Bruce Lee in "Enter the Dragon" and a martial arts karate studio owner and friend of Chuck Norris, a black belt competitor, a real estate businessman, and an author of "Who's who in the Martial Arts" in 1975.

Bill Wallace – Karate, Boxing, Undefeated Kickboxing Champion – Bill was known as "Superfoot" and is an undefeated PKA middleweight champion with a 23-0 record. He is highly sought after to give seminars all over the world. Bill is an actor in several films and is the author of three books.

Jim Butin is available for consulting and lectures in person or online.

Jim Butin, Grand Master 10th Degree Black Belt

Beyondthefighting@gmail.com

1-405-202-8701

Visit the website...
beyondthefighting.com